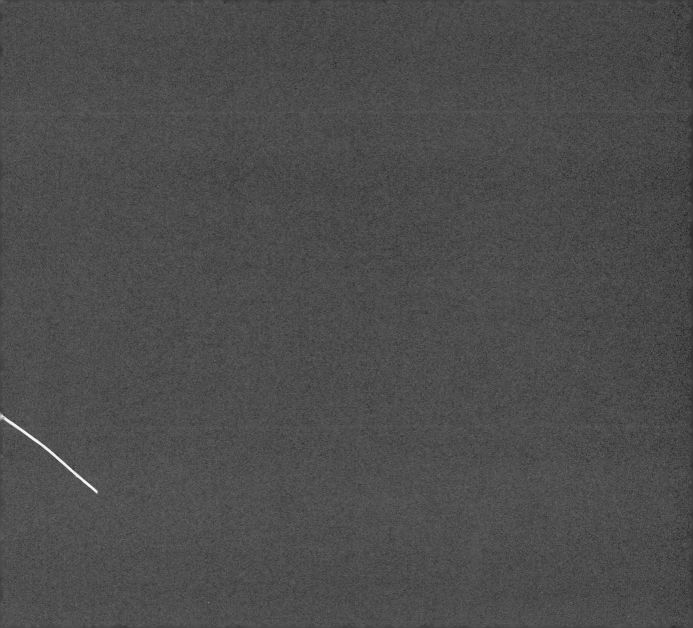

# The Extraordinary Life
### of
## His Holiness
### the
## Fourteenth Dalai Lama

# An Illuminated Journey

Narrated by the Dalai Lama

Text and Art by Rima Fujita

Wisdom

Wisdom Publications
199 Elm Street
Somerville, MA 02144 USA
wisdomexperience.org

*Library of Congress Cataloging-in-Publication Data*
Names: Bstan-'dzin-rgya-mtsho, Dalai Lama XIV, 1935– author. | Fujita, Rima, author, illustrator.
Title: The extraordinary life of His Holiness the fourteenth Dalai Lama: an illuminated journey / narrated by the Dalai Lama; text and art by Rima Fujita.
Description: Somerville, MA: Wisdom Publications, [2021] | Audience: Grades 4–6
Identifiers: LCCN 2020040710 (print) | LCCN 2020040711 (ebook) |
ISBN 9781614297499 (hardcover) | ISBN 9781614297642 (ebook)
Subjects: LCSH: Bstan-'dzin-rgya-mtsho, Dalai Lama XIV, 1935– —Juvenile literature. |
Dalai lamas—Biography—Juvenile literature. | Tibet Region—Biography—Juvenile literature.
Classification: LCC BQ7935.B777 A3 2021 (print) | LCC BQ7935.B777 (ebook) | DDC 294.3/923092 [B]—dc23
LC record available at https://lccn.loc.gov/2020040710
LC ebook record available at https://lccn.loc.gov/2020040711

ISBN 978-1-61429-749-9    ebook ISBN 978-1-61429-764-2

25 24 23 22 21      5 4 3 2 1

Cover design by Gopa & Ted 2. Interior design by Katrina Damkoehler.

Printed on acid-free paper that meets the guidelines for permanence and durability of the Production Guidelines for Book Longevity of the Council on Library Resources.

Printed in Malaysia.

I have faced many difficulties in my life, but I am quite happy.
I truly believe that the ability to be happy is in everyone's nature.

TENZIN GYATSO,
His Holiness the Fourteenth Dalai Lama

# Contents

# Foreword by
# His Holiness the Dalai Lama

Although I was born in a remote village in Tibet, I have spent most of my life in exile in India. Despite the terrible tragedies that befell Tibetan people, we have managed to re-establish our institutions in exile with great help from the Indian government, organisations and many individuals around the world.

Soon after our arrival in India in 1959, we introduced democracy in our Tibetan community in exile. In May 2011, I devolved my political authority to the elected leadership.

The very purpose of our life is to serve others and I remain committed to this path. It is through compassion, concern for the well-being of others we must endeavour to solve our human problems in a spirit of mutual concern and reconciliation. I have been devoting my efforts at contributing to the improvements of the society at large in whatever small a way, and to a more compassionate and peaceful world.

I am happy that Rima Fujita has created this short pictorial book on my life. I hope its readers will gain some inspiration to tread the path of nonviolence and compassion.

The Dalai Lama
7 October 2020

# 1: Birth

I grew up in Tibet at a time when people were free. Many were nomads and they lived wherever they wanted. My country had vast lands with lush green fields. Ever present on the horizon were white mountains covered with never-melting caps of snow and cascades of icy water. Wild animals were not afraid of humans because hunting was strictly prohibited.

There was a humble little village called Taktser in the northeast of Tibet with golden barley fields surrounded by rolling hills, green forests, and wide prairies. Juniper and poplar trees dotted the landscape, and peaches, apricots, walnuts, and berries grew everywhere, together with sweet-smelling flowers of many different shades. I was born in this beautiful farming village.

When I was born, in the summer of 1935, two crows came every morning and perched on the roof of my house. The same thing happened at the birth of the other Dalai Lamas of the past: the Seventh, Eighth, and Twelfth in particular.

My family was far from rich, but I was raised by loving parents in a loving environment. My father had a short temper, but he loved horses and he spent much of his time taking care of them. My mother was a very kind woman. She was the first person to teach me compassion.

She would often place me in a basket and churn butter while I lay at her side. I loved playing with the chickens and imitating them. *"Cluck, cluck!"* I would call—and then burst into laughter. I also enjoyed collecting chicken eggs with my mother. These are vague details but a few of my finest and earliest memories, which I still treasure to this day.

My family called me Lhamo Dhondup, meaning "Wish-Fulfilling Deity."

# 2: How I Was Discovered

I am the Fourteenth Dalai Lama. When the Thirteenth Dalai Lama passed away, a search team began looking for his new incarnation based on the instructions that he had left behind.

One day, Tibet's regent Reting Rinpoche had visions in the holy lake, Lhamoi Latso, one of which was the three letters, *ah*, *ka*, *ma.*

Later, when I was found near Kumbum monastery at Taktse, it became quite clear what those three letters meant. *Ah* stood for Amdo, *Ka* for Kumbum, and *Ma* probably hinted at my name.

Of the three search parties, the one that was sent to Amdo in the east finally found their way to my home in Taktse. In some ways, this very special holy lake is like a television screen: throughout its history, there have been many episodes of people seeing sacred visions on its surface!

The search team pretended to be travelers and stayed at our house. Kewutsang Rinpoche, the leader of the team, was disguised as a servant, while the real servant wore a monk's robes. They played with me to observe my behavior.

Although it was my first time meeting Kewutsang Rinpoche—and in spite of his disguise in servants' clothes—I knew his name without having been told what it was.

I also grabbed and pulled the mala he was wearing on his neck and said, "This is mine! This is mine!" That mala used to belong the Thirteenth Dalai Lama, and so I recognized it.

When they were departing I cried and said to them, "Please take me with you!"

Even before their arrival, I used to tell my family, "I am going to Lhasa! I'm going to Lhasa!" and pretend to be packing my bags.

Packing for Lhasa was one of my favorite childhood games.

I was two years old at the time.

# 3: Enthronement

After a while the search team came back again to conduct a more formal investigation. This time, Kewutsang Rinpoche was in his own robes, and the servant was dressed as a servant.

They brought several personal items that used to belong to the Thirteenth Dalai Lama. They added other similar objects to those that belonged to the Thirteenth Dalai Lama, to see if I could recognize the right ones.

"Which ones are yours?" they asked me.

I picked only the ones that belonged to the Thirteenth Dalai Lama.

The search team returned to Lhasa and the Tibetan Government officially confirmed my recognition that I was to be enthroned as the Fourteenth Dalai Lama.

I was only four years old.

# 4: Preparation for Lhasa

Needless to say, my parents were shocked.

My older brother had already been recognized as a rinpoche and was living at Kumbum Monastery nearby, so my parents thought it was possible that I could be another high lama, but they had never dreamed that I could be the Dalai Lama.

I was very happy, and I remember it very well.

I had always wanted to go to Lhasa and my dream was coming true.

Before moving to the Potala Palace in Lhasa, I was separated from my parents and placed for a time at Kumbum Monastery, without them.

Although my oldest brother was a rinpoche at this monastery, life there was very difficult for a small child like me.

When I made mistakes that were rather natural for a three-year-old, I was punished, sometimes painfully.

My only comfort was a gentle old monk who was one of my brother's teachers.

Once in a while, he would take me on his lap, wrap me in his robe, and give me dried apricots.

# 5: Life at the Potala

As a naughty four-year-old boy, I was officially enthroned as the Dalai Lama in 1940, and my name was changed from Lhamo Dhondup to Tenzin Gyatso. I began to live in the Potala Palace.

The Potala Palace was a huge, dark and very cold place. It was so big that you would never really know how many rooms were there.

On the walls were many murals, and statues of deities and the previous Dalai Lamas were everywhere. To a small child, they looked rather austere and sometimes even scary.

I had no friends of my age.

The only friends I had were sweepers and cooks in the palace. Although they were adults, they played with me with genuine laughter—but even they sometimes got angry with me.

They treated me as a true friend, not as the highest holy lama of Tibet.

There was a game we played often: you would place a flower or stone (or sometimes a cookie) some feet away and then race to get it first. When it was a flower, they used to say, "Oh, let His Holiness win," and they would let me get the flower. But if it was a cookie, they would run so seriously to get it and would not let me win at all!

My parents lived near the Potala, but I did not get to see them very often. When my mother visited me with all my favorite dishes that she had cooked, I would not share with anyone, perhaps out of loneliness, and would eat them all by myself. Then I normally ended up with bad stomachaches.

While lying in bed in the dark, the paintings of the deities on my walls looked even scarier, and I felt frightened. My only savior was the little mouse who would come down to drink the butter from the butter lamps every night. I felt happy when I saw him. He was my only companion and brought me temporary but instant comfort. I was quite lonely.

# 6: Childhood

As a student I was lazy.

My older brother, Lobsang Samten, and I studied together often—and were sometimes very naughty. As was the custom in Tibet at the time, our teachers had two different "whips" they told us were for particularly naughty monks: a purple whip for my brother and a yellow whip for me. Yellow is supposed to be a "sacred" color, so they made a special, yellow, "holy whip" for the Dalai Lama.

However, I found out that even though the colors were different, the pain you would receive was exactly the same.

You can imagine how disappointed I was!

Since I did not have friends of my age to play with, I spent a lot of time alone exploring the numerous gifts I received from around the world. The gifts were kept in the storage rooms at the Potala.

I especially enjoyed driving one of the imported classic cars inside the palace grounds.

I also liked to take apart and then reassemble watches. And when I did, time would just fly by.

I loved watching foreign movies and

news clips using a film projector. It was refreshing to watch them because there were hardly any foreigners in Tibet back then, and this way I got a sense of the world beyond Tibet.

One of my other daily routines was to gaze at the city of Lhasa and its surrounding Himalayan mountains through the big telescope on my balcony.

What caught my special attention were the prisoners. Chained by their feet, they eagerly performed repeated prostrations, facing toward me all day. It broke my heart and I hoped to release them one day.

One day, Lobsang Samten, my third brother, who had become a monk, was to leave the Potala Palace. My teachers and confidants thought I was depending on him too much and they believed it would be best for me if he went away.

I do not have to say how sad I felt losing the only emotional support I had from a family member.

# 7: Adolescence

In 1949 the People's Liberation Army gained control in China and began to aggressively pressure Tibet.

It was at this time in 1950 that I was forced to assume full political power of my country. I began my serious studies at age six, but most of my knowledge was related to Buddhist philosophy and I had no idea about politics or world affairs.

My predecessor, the Thirteenth Dalai Lama, took political power at the age of eighteen, so I insisted on doing the same. But I had no choice. Tibet was in such serious danger that I could not afford to wait any longer.

I was fifteen years old.

It was not easy for me to make decisions in politics as the head of state. I asked everyone around me for advice—and not only my teachers and confidants but also the sweepers and the cooks.

However, I always had to rely on myself in the end.

To help me make decisions, I would perform a *Mo,* which is a traditional Tibetan divination system that uses a set of dice.

From my own experience, I know that its results are always accurate. Therefore I trusted it.

On March 10, 1959, thousands of Tibetans who were concerned about my safety surrounded the Potala as they had heard that the Chinese Army was about to come and capture me. The Chinese Army brutally repressed the uprising.

It is estimated that more than 1.2 million Tibetans died as a direct result of the Chinese occupation of Tibet. Those people sacrificed their lives to protect me and their country.

Since I knew that it was too dangerous to remain in Tibet, as the Chinese Army was about to invade at any moment, I was waiting for the right moment to escape.

I wanted to remain in Tibet—but what would happen to my people if I was captured by the Chinese or died?

I was forced to flee my home to a free country—and I committed myself to saving my country from outside of Tibet. I had no other choice.

But when was the right time to leave Tibet?

For three months I had been waiting patiently for a cue from the Nechung Protector, a deity that the Dalai Lamas have consulted for centuries in making important decisions. The Nechung Oracle—a person who specialized in communicating with the Nechung Protector—would go into a trance and then speak advice from the deity.

Whenever I asked Nechung if it was time to leave Tibet, he would always reply, "Not yet, wait."

I endured many days with increasingly unsettling emotions.

In the afternoon on March 17, Nechung went into trance and told me "Please leave. Please leave tonight." His body shook fervently when he said this, and I felt a strong emotion. I still cannot forget his sad face at that moment.

He looked anguished as tears poured continuously from his eyes like a waterfall.

At ten o'clock that night, I disguised myself in a soldier's uniform, carrying a rifle over my shoulder, and quietly left the Norbulingka, my summer palace where I had been taking refuge.

It was March 17, 1959.

# 8: Exile

I felt sad to leave behind all the faithful monks and servants such as cooks and sweepers who could not join me when I fled from Norbulingka.

I rolled up the *thangka* painting of Palden Lhamo, my protector deity, and kept it close to me throughout the entire journey. This made me feel safer, despite the dangers ahead. It was comforting.

I feel her presence watching over me even today, at this very moment!

My family and I headed toward India by foot and riding on yaks for fourteen days. The whole time we were guarded by Tibetan soldiers, fighters, and confidants. The Nechung Oracle gave us detailed instructions for the route we should take.

Nevertheless, the journey was filled with danger, as there were Chinese Army checkpoints all along the way.

Somehow, we were protected.

Once, when we had to pass near a group of Chinese soldiers, a sandstorm suddenly appeared and shielded us from their view.

Such wondrous events of great fortune happened several times along our journey.

On March 31, 1959, we reached the Indian border.

I was completely drained and was running a high fever, and my entire entourage, including the yaks and horses, was totally exhausted.

Still we felt great relief.

After escorting me to a free land, my guards were ready to return to Tibet. They told me that they wanted to fight for their country. I was so sad. We cried and said goodbye, feeling that we might never see each other again.

As I had feared, many of those brave fighters got captured by the Chinese Army on their way back and never made it home alive.

# 9: Home

In India, we were welcomed by Indian Prime Minister Jawaharlal Nehru.

I took up residence in a small Indian village called Dharamsala in the foothills of the Himalayas. In that village, I formed the Tibetan Government-in-Exile, and began building the infrastructure needed to preserve the Tibetan culture.

At this point, there were about eighty thousand Tibetan refugees in India, Nepal, and Bhutan. They had followed me, fleeing Tibet and crossing the border into India. My priority was to build shelters, schools, and hospitals for them.

The refugees lived outside in simple, shabby tents. They cultivated the barren soil that no one else wanted and worked hard at growing corn and wheat. Many worked on dangerous road construction sites. Men, women, and children all worked hard to survive, exchanging hard labor for little pay.

There were many orphans in Dharamsala who had lost their parents and families—some to the Chinese during the escape from Tibet, and some through construction accidents while they were working. I became a father figure to those children, and they placed all their hopes in me.

I was twenty-four years old.

Since then, I have been seeking international support for Tibet and her people's well-being through peaceful dialogue.

As a Buddhist, despite the differences in philosophies and traditions of different religious traditions around the world, I have been promoting ways to create peace and cultivate happiness within.

I have been able to do this work because—although I live in exile—I live in a country that is democratic and free.

# 10: Nobel Peace Prize

As I have often said, I am a simple Buddhist monk.

Nothing more, nothing less.

I am just another human being among billions of people on this earth.

However, the fact that the Nobel Committee decided to grant me the Peace Prize in 1989 means that they must have valued something I was doing. Of course, I was happy to receive such respected recognition.

Right after the award ceremony, a friend of mine just couldn't wait any longer to ask me, "So, what are you going do with the prize money?!" We laughed so hard about this together. But if you really want to know, I donated my prize money to various organizations.

*Ahimsa*, the Indian word for nonviolence, is my basic principle.

Violence only creates more violence.

The true and lasting solutions to the problems our planet faces can only be attained through peaceful dialogue, and it is the only reliable answer to the conflicts in the world.

I have been asking China to have a peaceful dialogue with me for the last sixty years—but they have not accepted my request.

# 11: Sixty Years in Exile

I am in my mid-eighties now.

My body is quite old now, but my brain is still sharp—this is probably due to my many years of meditation practice. I used to spend more than two-thirds of a year traveling abroad, but nowadays I spend more time here in India.

When I am at home, I enjoy my morning walks and looking at the beautiful flowers in my garden. The row of stout cherry trees at my residence produces exquisite blossoms every year. They are the result of the tiny saplings that I brought back from Japan fifty years ago—so they have seen most of my life in exile.

I love animals and I have had dogs as pets. However, when my beloved dog died I was so sad that I promised myself not to have pets again; I decided not to give another dog a name and think of her as "mine." When you name an animal and call it "your pet" you instantly create emotional attachment. Attachment creates suffering. Therefore, ever since, when I adopted a dog, I no longer named the dog, and I tried to care for the dog from a distance.

There are many wild monkeys in Dharamsala, and they live around my residence too. One day, I noticed that the monkeys were harassing a newborn baby bird up in a tree. I called one of my bodyguards and told him, "You don't have to look after me, but can you watch the baby bird and make sure that the baby bird is safe from the monkeys?" The bodyguard stood at the foot of the tall tree all day for several days protecting the baby bird for me.

Everyone wants to be happy. All sentient beings want to live safely and no one wants to suffer. We all have that wish. However, we as humans have the ability to cultivate happiness by training the mind.

This is because we are all born with the potential to achieve true happiness. The Buddha taught how to cultivate happiness.

What he taught more than twenty-five hundred years ago has been passed on for millennia and is still practiced by almost half a billion people today. Still, you do not have to be a Buddhist to practice Buddhism.

I am a Buddhist monk who began his serious Buddhist study at age six—but I am also a human being with feelings. So, of course I get angry and sad just like everyone else. When I feel sad I often visualize the Buddha in lotus position and myself sitting next to him. Then I lay my head on Buddha's left knee.

Somehow, this always eases my sadness and comforts me.

# 12: My Four Commitments

When my beloved tutor, Ling Rinpoche, passed away, I was deeply saddened.

I felt as if I had lost a solid rock to lean on to. Rinpoche was extremely weak for the last three months of his life, and I have no doubt that he kindly lived a few extra months for me, so that I could prepare myself to part from my loving teacher and father figure.

In the hot Indian weather, Rinpoche's body did not decay for thirteen days after his death. I again believe that he did this because he wanted to give me enough time to get used to my life without him, as I was in such pain and sorrow over his passing. So, rather than mourning day after day, I decided to focus my energy on my mission of serving others in order to meet his expectations toward me.

I was fifty-eight years old at the time.

Today, I have four major life commitments. The first is my commitment as a human being. We humans need to enhance the value of compassion, forgiveness, tolerance, contentment, self-discipline, and hope in the world.

My second commitment is to encourage harmony between the world's religious traditions. As a Buddhist practitioner I wish for mutual understanding between all the major religions. Every religion has its benefit and capacity to serve humanity. So, we should respect them since all aspire to foster compassion and other basic human values.

My third commitment is the issue of Tibet. This includes working to protect the Tibetan environment, as well as the identity and well-being of the Tibetan people, and preserving Tibetan culture and freedom of religion.

In 1959, due to the Chinese invasion, I was forced into a situation in which I had to flee Tibet and try to help my country from outside. Although physically I had left my homeland, my heart never left Tibet. My heart has always remained there. And the Tibetans inside of Tibet have inherited my spirit and maintained it for many years.

My fourth commitment is to revive the ancient Indian knowledge of how to achieve inner peace and happiness.

I feel that the education on ancient Indian knowledge should be done in a non-religious, secular way, without relating it to religion at all, and in this way, it will be relevant to everyone.

One of my other wishes is to promote a modern education system that values "emotional hygiene." This is an approach to education in which people emphasize paying attention to compassion, tolerance, and so on, instead of fueling negative emotions, such as anger, frustration, jealousy, fear, and anxiety. Along with secular ethics, I think this is very much needed in today's world, as it has been neglected for too long.

# 13: My Wish

Most babies are born with their eyes closed, but when I was born, both of my eyes were fully open. Perhaps this was due to my specific mission in this lifetime. Either way, I am committed to work for peace as long as I can. I think I may live up to 103 years of age.

And if the Tibetans still want the "The Dalai Lama system" to continue, I will come back in my next life to serve the Tibetans and humanity. Alternatively, I may appoint the next Dalai Lama, the fifteenth, while I am still alive. This has never happened before and traditionally you must die first in order to be "found" as your next rebirth.

However, as the situation in Tibet is critical, I think that it is wise to choose my successor before my death. In this way, we can avoid the confusion that will ensue as China most likely tries to advance its own candidate for the next Dalai Lama.

In the end, kindness is my religion.

As I said, the first person who taught

me compassion was my mother. My family was not rich, but whenever hungry people or travelers came to our house, my mother always offered them food with a smile on her face, even if she had nothing left for herself.

People often ask me wherever I go in the world, "What can we do for you? What do you want us to do?" My wish is only this: cultivate compassion.

We human beings are social animals and no one can live without love and compassion. I ask you to cultivate compassion because, by doing so, you will be happier. If you wish happiness only for yourself you will never be happy, because everything is interconnected and interdependent. You cannot be happy alone while others are suffering, because we are all one.

For as long as space remains, and for as long as sentient beings remain, until then may I too remain to dispel the misery of the world.

—SHANTIDEVA

# Afterword by Rima Fujita

I did not know who the Dalai Lama was until my late twenties, and I had no knowledge about Tibet until one night in 1993 when I heard a commanding voice in my dream say "Help Tibet now!" The next day I spent many hours at the New York Public Library on 42nd Street learning about Tibet and its tragic occupation for the first time in my life. This is how my "journey to Tibet" began.

At that time, I started to create and donate picture books for Tibetan refugee children to help them preserve their threatened language and culture. Practicing Tibetan Buddhism became an essential part of my life, and H. H. the Dalai Lama has come to be my lifetime hero and root guru. I have attended his teachings and public talks in New York, Tokyo, and India, and have been graced to have had repeated opportunities to be in his presence.

I had never dreamed that I would have the honor to be asked by one of his confidants to create a picture book of his incredible life story, and I cannot find words that describe how humbled I felt. Since there is a tradition in Tibetan Buddhism that a student writes a book about their teacher, I consider this book the most important work in my life, and I sincerely have put my entire heart into it.

There was a time, shortly after I began to consider how to approach this project, that I was struggling with discerning how to proceed. One night, I had a vivid dream that H. H. the Dalai Lama was sitting next to me. We were talking and laughing together, and suddenly he took my hand, held it gently, and smiled at me. After this dream, the project began to unfold smoothly.

Another exquisite confirmation came through Palden Lhamo, the personal protector deity of His Holiness. When a friend in Dharamsala found out that I had been working on a book about the Dalai Lama, she sent me a picture of His Holiness's thangka of Palden Lhamo. I downloaded the image and printed it out in order to put it on my drawing easel. Each day, I wanted to look at this powerful deity and be inspired.

As the paper came out from the printer I saw that Palden Lhamo was empty space, while everything else around her was there. I thought that something might have gone wrong with the printer, so I printed it again. The same thing happened: the deity was blank except for her surroundings. Puzzled, I printed something else to test, and everything came out perfectly.

Some Tibetan friends told me that this is not rare. When people take photos of depictions of Palden Lhamo, they often come out blank. I do not know what it meant in my case, but I took it as a sign that her presence was there. She was there to protect His Holiness and to protect anything to do with him, including my picture book of his extraordinary life.

I had more help and support in this book as well. Everyone at Wisdom Publications was so kind throughout the production. They proved themselves time and again to be divinely inspired. I cannot thank the entire team at Wisdom enough, and I feel so grateful to have worked with such compassionate people who actually apply their Buddhist practice to their daily life at work.

I especially thank H. H. the Dalai Lama for his example. I have witnessed with my own eyes for many years that his words and his actions always match. He is so honest and genuine. He is the smartest, most humble, kindest person I have ever encountered. How fortunate are we to be alive in the same era of H. H. the Dalai Lama and to be able to receive his direct teachings and precious wisdom!

As he is eighty-six years young today, his health and well-being are a concern to many of us. Currently he is a firm pillar that is supporting the Tibetan diaspora, holding them all together—but I worry about what will happen to Tibetans when His Holiness leaves his current body. Since the age of four, he has tirelessly worked for his people and for the global community by promoting compassion and the oneness of humanity.

I cannot stop hoping that his great lifetime of work and messages of peace will be passed on to Tibetans in order for them to unite and stand firmly. It is imperative for the global community to help Tibetans regain their basic human rights and to preserve their own identity through their freedom of language, culture, and religion. I love the Tibetan people. They are some of the kindest and most generous people I've met in my life.

I will certainly visit Tibet when His Holiness returns to his motherland after many decades. Until then, I will continue on the path of my "journey to Tibet," and treasure the wisdom and love that H. H. the Dalai Lama has shared with us.

# Acknowledgments

My deepest gratitude goes to those who supported me as I created this book (in alphabetical order):

His Holiness
    the Fourteenth Dalai Lama

Daniel Aitken
Tsewang Gyalpo Arya
Paul Barsky
Josh Bartok
Gopa Campbell
Tsetan Samdup Chhoekyapa
Ven. Geshe Tenzin Choephel
Ven. Gyaltsen Chophel
Ven. Amdo Choejor
Tenzin Choejor
Laura Cunningham
Katrina Damkoehler
Kat Davis
Yeshi Dolma
Kunchok Dorjee
Junji & Keiko Fujita

Mpho Tutu van Furth
Ben Gleason
Ed Glendinning
David Gordon
Etsuko Ito
Maho Kawachi
Amane Kitamura
Liaison Office
    of H. H. the Dalai Lama–Japan
Tony Lulek
Lungtok
Alexandra Makkonen
Andrea Miller
Kestrel Montague
Nancy Murray
Dhondup Namgyal
Nechung Dharmapala Center Sangha
Naomi Nodera
Michiyo Ohara

Ven. Paljor
Ryan Phan
Tsewang Phuntso
Chhime Rigzing
Eric Ripert
Tsetan Sadutshang
Nanako Sakai
Ven. Geshe Ngawang Sonam
Taryn Sue
Tenzin Taklha
Sonam Topgyal
Tenzin Tselha
Archbishop Desmond Tutu
Eli Wakamatsu
Ven. Tenzin Thokme Wangdu
Ogoto Watanabe
Kim Witherspoon
Naoko Yamaguchi
Sonam Zoksang

48

# About the Author-Artist

Rima Fujita was born in Tokyo, lived in New York City for thirty-two years, and now resides in Southern California. She graduated from Parsons School of Design and has exhibited her work internationally to much acclaim, gaining collectors around the world. Rima has won various awards internationally, and received special recognition from H. H. the Dalai Lama and Desmond Tutu at the International Peace Summit in Japan.

In 2001 Rima established Books for Children, an organization that produces children's books and donates them to children in need around the world. She has created seven children's books and has donated more than fifteen thousand books to the Tibetan children in exile.

Her books include *Wonder Garden*, *Wonder Talk*, *The Little Black Box*, *Simple Meditation*, *TB Aware*, *Save the Himalaya*, *Rewa*, *Tibetan Identity*, and *The Day the Buddha Woke Up*. Rima's works have been presented at Rubin Museum of Art (New York), the Tagore Gallery (New York and Beverly Hills), Tibet House (New York), Trace Foundation (New York), Isetan Art Gallery (Tokyo), Mingei International Museum (San Diego), and San Diego Museum of Art.

Her work can be seen online at rimafujita.com.

# What to Read Next from Wisdom Publications

**See You, Buddha**

*A Story in Playful Rhyme Inspired by
the Buddhist Sutras*

Josh Bartok
Illustrated by Demi

"A magical book. Poetic, playful, and psychologically
adept." —Sumi Loundon Kim, author *Sitting Together:
A Family-Centered Curriculum on Mindfulness, Meditation, and Buddhist Teachings*

**The Compassionate Life**

His Holiness the Dalai Lama

"This sorely needed prescription for sanity and kindness in the world is unbelievably simple and unbelievably important, and therefore a practice worthy of our
wholehearted commitment." —Jon Kabat-Zinn, author
of *Wherever You Go, There You Are*

**The Day the Buddha Woke Up**

Andrea Miller
Illustrated by Rima Fujita

"Rima Fujita brings the Buddha's life vividly alive for
us with her exquisite sense of style and color, and her
heartfelt appreciation of his gifts to the world. Read-
ing it is a lovely experience, one people young and old
should treasure." —Robert Thurman

**Prince Siddhartha**

*The Story of Buddha*

Jonathan Landaw and Janet Brooke

"A must-have on the list of any parent interested in
exposing a child to the basics of Buddhism."
—*Beliefnet.com*

# About Wisdom Publications

Wisdom Publications is the leading publisher of classic and contemporary Buddhist books and practical works on mindfulness. To learn more about us or to explore our other books, please visit our website at wisdomexperience.org or contact us at the address below.

Wisdom Publications
199 Elm Street
Somerville, MA 02144 USA

We are a 501(c)(3) organization, and donations in support of our mission are tax deductible.

Wisdom Publications is affiliated with the Foundation for the Preservation of the Mahayana Tradition (FPMT).